Mastering the Art of Communication

Mastering the Art of Communication

Your Keys to Developing a More Effective Personal Style

by Michelle Fairfield Poley

SkillPath Publications
Mission, Kansas

Editor: Kelly Scanlon

Cover and Book Design: Rod Hankins

Library of Congress Catalog Card Number: 95-71717

ISBN: 1-878542-34-6

10   9   8   7   6   5   4   3   2   95   96   97   98   99

Printed in the United States of America

For Ross, Eleanor, Michael,
Jonathan and Robin

With love.

CONTENTS

Chapter ONE

What Makes a Great Communicator?

Before you read this book, take a moment to answer a couple of important questions:

1. Name two people you consider great communicators.

   A. _____

   B. _____

2. What makes them great communicators?

   A. _____

   B. _____

Participants in communication skills training programs who are asked these same questions provide some interesting answers. There are always a few names that show up over and over—people such as John F. Kennedy, Martin Luther King, Ronald Reagan, Barbara Bush, Johnny Carson, Leo Buscaglia, Oprah Winfrey, and Robin Williams, for example. Other participants mention people from their personal lives—mothers, fathers, husbands, wives, co-workers, teachers, and friends. But no matter *who* the participants put on their lists, their *reasons* for putting them there are generally the same. Each of these candidates:

- Is a good listener.

- Involves the listener.

- Injects humor.

- Uses clear body language.

- Is enthusiastic.

- Doesn't talk down to the listener.

- Builds rapport.

Only very occasionally does someone say, "I admire that communicator because he has a great vocabulary." And even less frequently does anyone say, "Gosh, she really uses *great grammar,* doesn't she?" And only once in a blue moon does anyone make any reference at all to great *content.*

Yet many people expect to become better communicators by improving their technical language skills. Certainly grammar, vocabulary, and syntax are all elements of effective communication. So is clear, powerful content. It's just that most listeners don't notice those things until *after* you've won them over with your style and rapport skills.

For communication to be truly effective, it needs to be clear and correct. But more important, the message must be positioned in a way that *inspires* or *motivates* the listener (or reader) to tune in.

In this book, you'll find exercises and worksheets designed to help you hone your skills in clarity, correctness, and effectiveness. Work with them and notice your progress. Consider keeping a "Communication Effectiveness Journal" for the next few months as you practice your new skills (see the sample journal sheet provided at the end of this book).

Most of all, ask a few of your closest friends to help you by participating with you in some of the exercises. No one communicates in a vacuum. By its very nature, effective communication always includes others. Include them now and watch your skills grow!

Now, give the communication skills exercise on the next page a try. Consider it a pretest. Then check your answers with those on page 7. Any surprises?

4

EXERCISE 1

Testing Your Communication Savvy

1. When Uncle Henry died, he left his entire estate to be equally divided between John, Patty and Jack and Mark.

   How much of that estate did Patty receive?

   A. 33%

   B. 25%

   C. 16.5%

   D. It depends on how generous Jack is.

2. Sandy showed Mark how to spot his errors quickly.

   Which of these two statements is true:

   A. Sandy showed Mark this new skill quickly—it took her only 10 minutes.

   B. Mark now finds his errors much more quickly than before.

3. You are talking to a co-worker about an important project you've been working on. In the middle of the conversation, while you are speaking, your co-worker rolls her eyes.

   What does that mean?

   A. She is bored.

   B. She is disgusted.

   C. She wears contact lenses and her eyes just became uncomfortably dry.

   D. All the above.

   E. You can't really know for sure.

4. Jason prides himself on his ability to avoid all the politics in his office. He is responsible, capable, and diligent. His co-workers don't know him very well because he never goes to company get-togethers and stays pretty much to himself.

   Jason will probably be promoted soon.

   A. True

   B. False

5. You notice that when you and your boss talk, she tends to stand closer to you than you are comfortable with.

   An assertive method of dealing with this would be to:

   A. Take a step even closer.

   B. Take a step back.

   C. Stay where you are.

   D. Mention it.

6. A plethora is:

   A. An Egyptian python.

   B. A subterranean flaw, usually found in polar areas.

   C. A lot of something.

   D. A chronic lack.

7. In 1973, a graduate researcher at Harvard University discovered that 29 percent of the general public in the United States began each day by looking in the mirror and saying, "What can I do to be truly *impossible* today?"

   A. True

   B. False

8. The purpose of communication is:

   A. To send a message to the receiver.

   B. To impress the receiver.

   C. To inspire or motivate the receiver.

   D. None of the above.

9. A human being can change the intensity of an emotional response by calling that emotion something different.

   A. True

   B. False

10. Especially in business communication, the communicator should always put the most important idea at:

   A. The beginning.

   B. The end.

   C. Both the beginning and the end.

Testing Your Communication Savvy

ANSWERS

1. Any of these scenarios is possible. There are several ways to read this sentence. First, the word *between* is used with only two people or things. "Among" is used with three or more. Second, the lack of a serial comma creates ambiguity. The serial comma is the comma that some people use in a series of items before the word *and*. Should each of the beneficiaries receive a quarter of the estate? Should John receive 33 percent; Patty and Jack combined, 33 percent; and Mark, 33 percent? Or should John receive a third; Patty a third; and Jack and Mark combined, a third? In the middle example, how much Patty receives would either be 16.5 percent (half of 33 percent), or depend on how well she works out a deal for her share with Jack. Notice that if the serial comma had been used in this sentence, there would be no ambiguity.

2. Who knows? The word *quickly* is an adverb, and there are two verbs in this sentence. Because *quickly* was not placed right next to one of those verbs, the intended message is unclear. Better alternatives:

   Sandy quickly showed Mark how to spot his errors.

   Sandy showed Mark how to quickly spot his errors. (Yes, this sentence contains a split infinitive. You'll find more information about when it's okay to bend the rules of grammar in Chapter 4.)

3. E. You just can't know for sure. Nonverbal language is *very* powerful, but often misread.

4. FALSE. Playing office "politics" is almost always a necessary element of a promotion. They don't have to be

the negative, backstabbing kind though. Actually, *truly* effective political skills are just excellent communication skills.

5. D. Talking about it is truly the assertive response. Taking a step closer is *aggressive;* taking a step back is *submissive;* and staying where you are is not conducive to effective communication—you'll have trouble paying attention because of your discomfort.

6. C

7. FALSE. Did you even need to look this one up?

8. Most often, A. But C can't hurt. B is okay, but only when A and C already exist.

9. TRUE. "I am *furious*" doesn't mean the same thing to your psyche as "I'm peeved." Call your emotional state something different and you will automatically change your inner response.

10. Definitely A. Never B. C is recommended for longer speeches.

Chapter

TWO

Clarity: Your Top Priority

Have you ever been the victim of *mis*communication?

Try this simple test: In a small box below this paragraph, you will see a word. The split second you read that word, notice the picture that develops in your mind. Ready?

dog

Did you get a picture of a dog? Or did you get a picture of the three letters *d*, *o*, and *g* next to each other inside a box?

Not many people see the letters. (There *are* always a few readers who see a cat though. If you did, don't worry!)

This, in fact, is how communication is *meant* to work. Words are not the meaning—they are only the symbols of the meaning. When I thought of a dog, the first picture I got was of my old dog Marhalt Poley. Marhalt was the best dog I ever had. He was half Irish wolfhound and half English sheepdog—very tall and very shaggy. At Christmas time, I used to dress him up in a Santa Claus outfit, complete with hat, cape, and red and green pom-poms (with jingle bells in them) on his paws. (If you've ever had a big dog, you can imagine how much he liked that costume.) His favorite thing to do was to go out into the backyard and gnaw on tree stumps that were still in the ground.

Is that the picture you got of a dog when you read the word inside the box? Are you beginning to see how miscommunication generally happens?

Our thoughts always start as pictures. It's only when we need to communicate those thoughts to other people that we are forced to translate those pictures into words. And, of course, that's where miscommunication often happens. Exercise 2 will help you understand this even more.

EXERCISE 2

Communication or Miscommunication?

What does the word *love* mean to you? Write down the first ten things you think of.

_____

_____

_____

_____

_____

_____

_____

_____

_____

_____

Just for fun, here are the lists of what *love* means to several other people who responded to this exercise.

Example 1:

commitment	tenderness
acceptance	giving
growing	hard work
unselfishness	caring
playfulness	friendship

Example 2:

unselfish	undeserved
forgiving	physical gratification
passion	respect
sharing	companionship
limitless	hate

Example 3:

affection	sharing
commitment	friendship
support	laughter
expectations	forgiveness
wholeness	pride

Now, think of the last two or three people you said "I love you" to. Ask them for the first ten things they think of when they see or hear the word *love*. Have you ever wondered why your loving relationships sometimes don't work out the way you thought they should? Is it starting to make sense? Are you beginning to get an idea of the challenge involved in ensuring the *clarity* of communication?

The fact is, we are all victims of The Transmission Model of Communication:

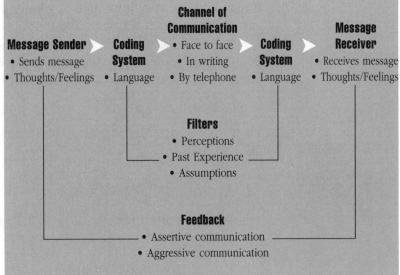

Communication starts as a picture in the sender's brain and ends as a picture in the receiver's brain. There are encoding and filtering processes on both ends involving the language itself, the type of communication (e.g., written or face-to-face), as well as the past experiences and perceptions of both parties. Actually, it's probably a miracle that people ever understand each other. Neither the sender nor the receiver is ever in total control of the effectiveness of the message. It is always a shared responsibility.

But here is the Cardinal Rule of Effective Communication:

> *It is always the sender's responsibility to make a particular communication as clear as possible for the receiver.*

The reason for this rule is apparent: Until the receiver receives the message, it is the sender who cares the most about that message. Certainly, once the receiver understands the message, it may become very important to him or her. But your receivers can't know—much less care about—something they don't yet know. And most receivers in today's world are *overcommunicated* to anyway. They don't have much time—or energy—to try to decode a message that is too complex.

Here, then, are the six keys to clarity:
1. Always use the simplest word available.
2. Avoid indefinite words.
3. Isolate your most important ideas into separate statements.
4. Follow the rules—within reason.
5. Refine your nonverbal skills.
6. Check in with the receiver periodically.

KEY ONE

Always use the simplest word available.

Sometimes, when you use a complex word, you lose clarity. Joe, a lawyer for a bank that recently purchased a smaller bank, was sent by his boss to the new bank's monthly management meeting. "Go facilitate at the meeting," he was told. While he was on the way there, his boss called the other bank and told the manager Joe would be arriving: "I've sent him to facilitate."

"Great," the manager of the new bank said. "We'll give him a doughnut when he gets here."

That wasn't Joe's understanding of the word *facilitate,* so plenty of long-lasting, negative feelings were sparked when he arrived and assumed control of the meeting.

The fact is, words like *facilitate, cognizant, ameliorate,* and *apprise* are not clear. It doesn't really matter what the dictionary says they mean—most listeners and readers don't listen or read with a dictionary in their laps. So they can't double-check the meanings of all large words on the spot. Nor should they have to. Most people develop their understanding based on their *impressions* of what those words mean. And that's where problems arise. Sometimes, as in the case about Joe, those meanings are not the same.

Here's an important corollary to using the simplest word available: Always use every word you need to be clear. But trim the excess.

Some examples of how to be brief but clear appear in the accompanying chart, "Brevity That Works."

16

Brevity That Works

Wordy	Better
a large number of	many
a majority of	most
a sufficient number	enough
at this time	now
by the time that	when
called attention to the fact	reminded
due to the fact that	because
exactly alike	identical
except in a small number of cases	usually
for the purpose of	for/to
for the reason that	because
in accordance with	by/under
in addition to	also/besides
inasmuch as	because/since/as
in the event that	should
in view of the fact that	considering
it would appear that	it seems
make a purchase	buy
make contact with	meet
on behalf of	for
on two different occasions	twice
pertaining to	about
pursuant to	following
since the time when	since
subsequent to	after/following
there is no doubt that	doubtless/no doubt
until such time as	until
within the realm of possibility	possible/possibly
with regard to	about

KEY TWO

Avoid indefinite words.

Many words fail to communicate a clear message because they are vague. Have you ever seen words and phrases like these?

Substantial savings	*Strong* likelihood
Highly recommended	*Very good* response
I'll call you *soon*	*As soon as possible*
Quick service	A *good* employee
Frequently used	*Effective* sales representative
Satisfied client	A *nice* person

What do the italicized words really mean? More important, do they mean the same thing to the sender as they do to the receiver? Probably not.

Fortunately, there are two remedies for this lack of clarity:

1. Be specific.

    Vague:

    John, I need these figures from you as soon as possible.

    Clear:

    John, I need these figures from you by 3 o'clock Friday afternoon so Andrea can review them before she leaves town Saturday morning.

    Which one of those statements would more likely get the figures to you by your deadline?

2. Paint a picture.

Vague:

Mary had been a good employee.

Clear:

I don't know what we'd do without Mary! She comes in an hour early every Friday just to make sure that everyone's reports are ready for the weekly staff meeting. She often works through her lunch hour to keep up with all the extra work the department head piles on her, and she never complains about it. Everyone in the organization counts on her to fill in when there's other business to be handled. Plus, I usually see her still working at her computer when I finally leave at 7:00 each evening.

Granted, most of us probably have another name for Mary (saint and workaholic are just a couple that may come to mind), but which of those two explanations of her employment would more likely earn her a raise?

 **KEY THREE**

Isolate your most important ideas into separate statements.

The best way to emphasize an idea (and, therefore, to ensure clarity) is to make sure the listener or reader has been properly "set up" to understand it.

Notice the difference between these two statements:

Example 1: According to last week's report, business is getting better and I'm sure glad about that because if things hadn't turned around within the next month, we would have been forced to make massive layoffs and possibly to modify or discontinue some of our most popular benefits programs, most likely the health insurance and 401K plans and people wouldn't have liked that at all.

Example 2: I just read last week's report. Business is getting better! I'm sure glad about that—if things hadn't turned around within the next month, we could have been facing some unpleasant situations. Management had discussed the possibility of massive layoffs and the modification of some of our most popular benefits packages (like health insurance and the 401K). People wouldn't have liked that at all.

Which of those two paragraphs more clearly communicates *all* the ideas it contains? Most readers would agree it is the second example. The pauses (shorter sentences with more frequent punctuation) give the receiver an opportunity to consider and mentally digest what has been presented and then prepare for what is still to come.

Make sure to break up your important ideas for your listeners and readers. It is one of the easiest ways to make your communication more clearly understood.

An important note: Obviously...too...many...pauses... will...bore...your listener...or reader...to tears...!

 **KEY FOUR**

Follow the rules—within reason.

Grammar rules will be discussed in more detail in Chapter 4. It's enough to say for now that the sole purpose of grammar rules is to make sure that both the sender and the receiver share an understanding of the way their language works. This common understanding helps them encode and decode *clearly* and *correctly* the message they are attempting to share.

It's useful to consider, though, that most readers and listeners don't do their reading and listening with a grammar guide in their laps, ready to double-check any nuance of the language they're not 100 percent sure they understand. Just as most people don't use a dictionary to look up words they're not familiar with, most receivers don't bother to check something that *sounds* like it makes sense. They'll simply respond to it based on what they think it means.

For this reason, another Cardinal Rule for Effective Communication states:

If you ever find yourself speaking or writing something that sounds awkward to you, be sure to reword it. You already know what you're trying to say, but your receiver doesn't. In fact, your receiver is relying on these words to effectively decode your message.

# KEY FIVE

Refine your nonverbal skills.

Nonverbal skills are so crucial to communication that they will be covered in careful detail in Chapter 6. For now, here are the facts in a nutshell:

In any face-to-face communication, only 7 percent of the message the receiver receives is from the *words* the sender uses. Another 38 percent comes from the vocal quality (inflection, tone, pace, and so forth). The final component of communication—the largest component, incidentally—is body language. A full 55 percent of the meaning the receiver gets comes from the body language the sender uses!

Has this ever happened to you? Has anyone ever said something to you that you just didn't believe or trust? What was their vocal quality like? How about their body language? Did it match the words that person was saying? Probably not.

Here's an example: Mary welcomed Bob, a co-worker, into her office. Mary's arms were crossed tightly across her chest, and she wore a look of absolute disgust on her face. Her vocal quality was bored and disgusted. Her words? "I'm delighted to see you." True or false?

Your ability to communicate clearly depends on your ability to communicate *congruently*. This means that your words must match your vocal quality must match your body language. When faced with an incongruent message, your receiver evaluates your message *first* with your body language, *second* with your vocal quality, and *last* with your words.

This fact, by the way, is the reason so many communicators have a much more difficult time *writing* than they do *talking*. In writing, there isn't a nonverbal message to fall back on.

 **KEY SIX**

Check in with the receiver periodically.

Communication does not occur in a vacuum. Even if the sender is sending at 100 percent, the communication won't necessarily be 100 percent effective. The receiver's ability to decode the message must also be factored in.

The most reliable way to determine the effectiveness of a communication exchange is to *ask*. Have your listeners or readers explain back to you, in their own words, what you were communicating. Listen with an open mind and then correct, modify, or congratulate—whichever is appropriate.

Remember: The purpose of communication is to send a message, as clearly as possible, from one person to another. Your message starts as a picture in your brain. Your aim is to *duplicate* that picture in your receiver's brain. This is the true meaning of clarity.

Chapter
THREE

Positioning Your Message

The concept of positioning* has its foundation in one of the basic rules of selling: In order to sell a product effectively, the seller must communicate *what's in it for the buyer.*

This theory is also critical to the success of communication.

There are four keys to effectively positioning your message. Notice how much better your receivers respond to your messages when you use these techniques.

---

*The concept of positioning was originally developed and discussed by two marketing specialists, Al Reis and Jack Trout. They are the authors of several books on the topic, aimed primarily at people involved in sales, advertising, and marketing.

Here, then, are the four keys to effectively positioning your message:

1. Think of every communication as an opportunity to *sell* yourself to the receiver.

2. Remember that most receivers are bombarded with communication.

3. Understand the receiver's needs and point of view.

4. Choose your words carefully. Avoid those that trigger negative reactions.

 **KEY ONE**

Think of every communication as an opportunity to sell yourself to the receiver.

Think about it: Isn't most communication a sales opportunity? Certainly, it's not always hard sales—of a definite product or service. But isn't it sometimes sales of your image?

Or sales of your reputation?

Doesn't what and how you communicate add to your receiver's knowledge and impression of you?

 **KEY TWO**

Remember that most receivers are bombarded with communication.

Positioning also becomes important to a communicator who understands the concept of an overcommunicated receiver. Indeed, in this very busy world, *all* senders are involved in a sales transaction—whether they realize it or not.

We are bombarded with information from all our senses every minute of the day. We can't and don't pay attention to all of it. If we did, we'd go insane.

Has this ever happened to you? Has a co-worker ever tried to talk to you while you were finishing up an important project? Has your husband, wife, or partner ever told you all about his or her day—before you'd effectively wound down from your own?

Our brains are selective by nature. As you read these words, stop for a moment and think about the little toe on your left foot. What is it feeling right now? Can you feel it immediately? Or does it take a moment to tune in? Once you have tuned in, notice the sensation coming from it. Is it warm, cold, achy, numb, or what? No matter what it is feeling, does this mean that it is just *now* that your left little toe has begun to send sensory impulses to your brain? Of course not. That little toe has been sending messages to your brain ever since it was created. But *how often have you been listening to it?!*

Unless our brains recognize a compelling reason to pay attention to a message, we most likely *won't* pay attention. Actually, this is a useful function of the brain. If we *did* pay attention to everything, we'd soon become overloaded, and unable to process *anything*. Give your receiver a *reason* to pay attention.

KEY THREE

Understand the receiver's needs and point of view.

To be an effective communicator, you must help your receiver tune in to your message by positioning it *for that receiver's needs and point of view.* In order to do that, you must *understand* your receiver.

Read through the examples below. Which of Marie's positioning tactics do you think would more effectively help her achieve her objective? She is asking her boss for a raise.

Example 1: Jane, I really need this raise because my husband got laid off last week and we have lots of bills to pay. It would make me feel a lot better about working for you if I knew you and the organization cared about me.

Example 2: Jane, in the past six months, I've doubled the production coming out of this department. I think there's a way we could triple it. I know that your boss has been delighted with our progress so far and that you could be promoted because of it. Let's negotiate a compensation package for me right now that's based on our future progress. We could actually tie my increase to the increase in the department's production.

Example 3: Jane, I deserve this raise. If you don't give it to me right now, I'll have no option but to quit. I just won't tolerate any less.

As you evaluate the possibilities, remember the definition of *effective.* Not only should Marie's approach achieve her desired goal, it also must *maintain the relationship for the long term.*

In other words, in some cases, Example 1 and Example 3 could work to get Marie the raise. But what do they do to the long-term relationship with Jane and the company? Example 2 meets *both* criteria—it achieves her immediate goal of getting a raise and it preserves the long-term relationship.

It's true that a sender can't always know the receiver intimately, or even well. But when the receiver is a stranger, the sender should work hard to at least understand the *environment* he or she is sending the message into.

Exercise 3 contains a checklist for understanding your receiver in order to position your message effectively.

EXERCISE 3

Understanding Your Receiver to Position Your Message

1. What is my goal in this communication?

_____

2. What is my ultimate goal in my relationship with this receiver?

_____

_____

3. What are my assumptions about this situation and this receiver?

_____

_____

4. Are those assumptions valid?

_____

_____

5. What's in it for the receiver?

_____

_____

6. What are the potential drawbacks for the receiver?

_____

_____

7. How can I overcome them?

_____

_____

1. What is my goal in this communication?

   To get a raise—10 percent a year

2. What is my ultimate goal in my relationship with this receiver?

   To maintain a positive, professional, friendly but assertive image

3. What are my assumptions about this situation and this receiver?

   The company doesn't want to give a raise right now.

4. Are those assumptions valid?

   Well...what if the person getting the raise more than paid for it in extra production?

5. What's in it for the receiver?

   Better image to her boss, because of increased work; more production

6. What are the potential drawbacks for the receiver?

   Spending the company's money!

7. How can I overcome them?

   Develop a detailed plan of my intent to increase my worth by increasing company's bottom line. Tie increases to that.

KEY FOUR

Choose your words carefully. Avoid those that trigger negative reactions.

Besides understanding your receiver's needs, you must carefully choose the words you use to position your message. In general, negative words turn listeners (and readers) off. Here are some of the more common words that trigger negative reactions:

No	Wrong
Not	Fail
Never	Failure
Couldn't	Fault
Wouldn't	Inadequate
Shouldn't	Inferior
Can't	Insist
Don't	Demand
Won't	Lie
Should	Misinform
Allege	Mistake
Claim	Neglect
Complain	Overlook
My lawyer	Business Writing Clichés
Error	Gobbledygook
Must	Jargon
Oversight	

Following that same idea, work hard to use words that make your receiver feel good. Here is a list of words that can win positive results:

Yes	Gladly
Admire	Happy
Respect	Grateful
Deserve	Gratitude
Agree	Pleasure
Benefit	Satisfy
Comfort	Thank you
Good	Value
Great	Welcome
Please	At no charge
Congratulations	Kind

Personal words

Clear words

Chapter
FOUR

Why Correctness Is Essential (Most of the Time)

Great communicators know that there are three main reasons why using the English language correctly is essential:

1. Incorrect use of the language gives the receiver of the communication a poor *image* of the sender.

2. Poor grammar, spelling, sentence structure, and pronunciation make the sender's message hard to understand.

3. Mistakes of form often alienate the receiver to the point that he or she actually *refuses* to take the sender seriously.

The purpose of business communication, whether written or spoken, is to inspire the receiver to *action*. Not necessarily to *physical* action, however. Action in business communication is often an *emotional* or *intellectual* response. The importance of correctness is that it so often influences the receiver's ability to understand and empathize with the sender—to experience a response. When the sender uses the language incorrectly, so that it is unappealing to the receiver, the receiver likely will not receive the message. And, of course, if the receiver doesn't receive the message, no action is possible.

Keep in mind that language is a means to an end, not an end in itself. Language is the formalized method society has developed to convey thoughts and ideas; therefore, mastery of the rules governing any language makes people confident of their ability to be heard and understood. Zacharias Rosner, the president of the well-respected Grammar Group, compares good grammar to good table manners: without either, one can never be truly confident. Before reading any further, try Exercise 4.

EXERCISE 4

Testing Your Mastery of Language

Here is an example of both correct and incorrect grammar, spelling, and sentence structure. Try to identify the errors—and allow yourself to react to them. After reading each sample, ask yourself:

- What is the sender's *intended* message?
- What message did I *receive?*
- What is my *image* of the sender?

1. The shipment will get their Tuesday. I hope its soon enough for you. (*There* and *it's* are correct. The spelling mistakes in this message, let alone the tone, will destroy the sender's image.)

2. Before reading the letter, the computer broke. (Too bad the computer missed that letter!)

3. Me and Mary really like the way the group are working together. (Mary and *I. Group* is a collective noun, so it requires an *is.*)

4. I didn't get the affect I was hoping for out of that experiment. (*Effect* is correct.)

5. Matt's performance has been improving steadily since the day we hired him. I wouldn't trade him. (Correct.)

6. Cindy read the report she write about the new division. I didn't understand all of it. She's not a very good writer. (Who's calling whom a poor writer?)

7. The principle at stake is that we simply can't improve on the quality of our product without costing our customers a bundle. (Very negative. Turns readers off.)

8. The principle at stake is the quality of our product. Do you think our customers will be willing to pay a few cents extra for a much improved container? (Same as #7, but positioned in a very positive way.)

On the following pages, you will be introduced to the four major areas of correctness important to writing and to speaking:

- Grammar

- Spelling

- Syntax (sentence structure)

- Pronunciation

You will also be given examples of both correct and incorrect forms. *Study* them. Allow yourself to *react* to them. Ask yourself whether the form of the communication has become anything more than a vehicle for the message. If it has, it is probably not serving the best needs of the sender.

Grammar

Grammar can be defined as the rules that govern the use of a language. Of course, every language has grammar. This book discusses *American English* grammar.

Why not just *one* set of grammar rules for the English language? Well, if you've ever spent time discussing the English language with someone from England, you can probably answer that question easily.

In America, our language is very forgiving—its rules bend according to our ability to use them correctly. This does not happen overnight. But careful communicators notice on a continuing basis that the rules of our grammar *change* with time. This is not as true in England. There, the King's English (or Queen's English) is the accepted style and the citizenry is expected to learn it.

Here's a common example. In America, periods and commas are placed *inside* closing quotation marks—no matter what.

> Ross said, "Let's get some lunch."

> They think Melissa is a "free-thinker."

In England, the rule is exactly opposite. Periods and commas always go *outside* the closing quotation marks:

> Ross said, "Let's get some lunch".

> They think Melissa is a "free-thinker".

Here's the reason for the difference: In America, when printers started using printing presses for the first time, they found that they had a physical problem placing periods and commas outside the quotation marks, especially when using a cursive script, which tilted to the right. At that time, printed copies were made by placing pieces of lead type on a tray and then mounting that tray onto a printing press. Printers found that when they placed the large quotation mark on the top of the line, the smaller period or comma on the bottom of the line (especially after a tilted letter) tended to fall off the tray while it was being mounted on the printing press. So printers started tucking them inside. And a rule of *American* English grammar changed.

So how, you ask, can a conscientious communicator stay on top of these changes? The best authority on correct English grammar is a grammar guide that you and your organization can agree on and trust. You see, to make the issue of correct grammar just a little more complicated, sometimes even accepted style guides disagree. Once you choose a style guide, follow it *consistently!*

When It's Okay to Bend the Rules of Grammar

Most important, your correct use of grammar should never interfere with your reader's or listener's ability to understand the message you are sending. In business communication especially, it is wise to avoid using any awkward-sounding sentences, whether they are grammatically correct or not. There are simply some rules business communicators have the license to bend.

Here, then, are the key rules of grammar that business communicators are generally licensed to bend in the interest of *clear* communication:

1. It's okay to end sentences with prepositions.
2. It's okay to split infinitives.
3. It's okay to begin sentences with conjunctions.
4. It's okay to reuse words.
5. It's okay to use simple contractions.
6. It's okay to use personal pronouns.

KEY ONE

It's okay to end sentences with prepositions.

Have you ever written or spoken a sentence like this?

> *Get her a towel to dry off with.*

And then, did you work hard to rearrange it?

> *Get her a towel with which to dry off.*

Oops! That's no better! *Off* is a preposition also. At this point, most communicators simply drop the offending word:

> *Get her a towel with which to dry.*

But now the message isn't as clear. What is she going to dry? Her car? The floor? Herself?

In business communication, it is the sender's *intended message* that must retain its integrity—no matter what. You can follow every rule of grammar on the books, but if you fail to communicate your message to a receiver, then you have failed as a communicator.

KEY TWO

It's okay to split infinitives.

If you're like most people, it's been quite a while since anyone bothered to tell you what an infinitive is, but you probably *have* recently heard never to split one. An infinitive is a verb form that begins with the word *to*. Hence, *to love, to trust, to go,* and *to work* are infinitive verb forms. And the advice of most grammarians has been to never put any other word between *to* and the verb. (Get it? to *never* put?)

But sometimes, to accurately and specifically convey meaning to a receiver, it's essential to split the infinitive. (*To accurately and specifically convey* is also a split infinitive.)

 **KEY THREE**

It's okay to begin sentences with conjunctions.

This "rule" dies hard. Most people have a near-inbred reaction against beginning a sentence with a conjunction. And who can blame them? Most grammar teachers have been very firm about this.

But remember: In business communication, it is far more important to convey information clearly and accurately than it is to follow some old rule no matter what the cost.

If you have any doubt about this, find a copy of the *Wall Street Journal*—any day's issue. On the front page alone, it's normal to find between twenty and forty sentences that begin with the words *and* or *but*. The editors realize they are communicating to readers who are *busy*. They therefore use sentences that are short (easy to understand) and that provide a logical flow from one sentence to the next.

By the way, have you noticed that some of the sentences in the past three paragraphs begin with conjunctions?

KEY FOUR

It's okay to reuse words.

Have you ever been told not to reuse the same noun in a paragraph? If you were writing a report about this book, for example, you would have been advised to call it a *book* the first time you referred to it, but then to think of something else to call it "so your reader won't get bored."

So what *could* you call this book? A handbook? A notebook? A guide?

Here's what happens:

> Dear Jane,
>
> Here's the book you asked me to send you. Notice that the handbook is filled with many interesting ideas. Most people enjoy using our notebook as a study tool. If you need any more copies of the guide, please let me know.

Poor Jane is wondering why the author of that letter forgot to enclose the *notebook, handbook,* and *guide!*

In business communication, never sacrifice clarity by changing words in midstream. When you mean *book,* say *book.*

KEY FIVE

It's okay to use simple contractions.

A basic tenet of business writing is to *write the way you talk*. Because most of us *talk* in contractions, it's perfectly understandable—and acceptable—to use them in our writing also.

A *simple* contraction is one that leaves no doubt in the receiver's mind as to its meaning. Words like *I'm, you're,* and *I'll* are actually less awkward to use than *I am, you are,* and *I will* in most sentences. Beware, though, of two types of less desirable contractions:

- Contractions that are negative words.

- Contractions that could easily be mistaken for possessives.

Negative words turn listeners and readers off—whether they are full words like *do not* or contractions like *don't*. Stay away from them.

Also be careful of constructions like this one:

The dog's black.

Most readers' instinctual response to that sentence would be "The dog's black *what?*" It looks like a possessive.

 **KEY SIX**

It's okay to use personal pronouns.

Many well-meaning business communicators try to avoid using the word *I,* especially in writing. They feel that it takes the emphasis away from the *we* of the organization they represent. But there are some situations when *I* is the only appropriate word.

How would you feel if you received this letter from an organization you had called?

> Dear Sir:
>
> Pursuant to our conversation, we are returning the enclosed contract to your organization.
>
> Please have it duly signed by the appropriate authority there, and then return it to us.
>
> Again, your phone call was appreciated. Please call us again if we can offer any further assistance.
>
> Sincerely,
>
> R.M. Gunnison

Did you notice that all references to the sender are in the plural form? "We are returning"…"return it to us"…"call us again"…"we can offer." And how about the sentence "Again, your phone call was appreciated." *By whom?*

It is plain to see that just a few changes could make this communication far more personal and far more *effective*.

Dear Lee,

Thank you for your phone call yesterday. Here is the contract I told you I'd send.

Please have Bill sign it, and then return it to me in the postage-paid envelope I've enclosed. I'll see that it gets into the proper file here.

Again, thanks for your call. Your sense of humor always makes it such a pleasure for me to handle your requests. Let me know if I can help you any further.

Sincerely,

Robin M. Gunnison

The days when an impersonal, stand-offish attitude impressed business people are gone. Be natural instead. Focus on the *you* in your message, but don't be afraid of the *I*.

Spelling

Have you ever received a piece of mail that was addressed to a misspelled version of your name? Did you throw it away without opening it?

Obviously, only communicators who commit their words to *writing* must worry about correct spelling. But what a responsibility it is!

The good news is that you don't have to be a "born speller" to confidently spell most words correctly. The best advice about spelling hasn't changed: When in doubt, look the word up in a dictionary.

Unfortunately, that's not always easy. Maybe you're too busy to stop writing. Maybe you can't find the word. Or maybe you don't have a dictionary.

One of those problems is simple to solve: Make sure you have a dictionary *and* keep it near your writing area.

As for other spelling problems, know one thing: You are working with the English language. And the English language has borrowed words from *many* different languages and cultures. The two largest sources are Latin (through French) and Anglo-Saxon. But there are also words with Greek and German origins—as well as a number of others.

Here's the bad news: the spelling rules of Latin, Anglo-Saxon, Greek, and German are all different. It's practically impossible for most of us to correctly spell every word we need to use the first time we are asked to spell it. How could we possibly know which rules to apply?

Here's the good news: You don't need to put yourself down any longer for being a "poor speller." Just learn some ways to remember the correct spellings of words so that you don't have to keep looking them up over and over.

Here are the five keys for finding and remembering the correct spelling of *any* word:

1. Use your computer spell-checker.

2. Use a thesaurus to find difficult-to-spell words.

3. Write your misspelled words *correctly* ten times, saying them aloud as you go.

4. Isolate your trouble spot in the word and find a gimmick to help you remember.

5. Keep a list of your own troublesome words.

KEY ONE

Use your computer spell-checker.

But *really* use it. Let it correct your words for you, and then take a moment to *absorb* the corrections it made. Most of us rely on our spell-checkers, but we don't really learn from them. Vow today to start paying more attention to yours.

An important note: Don't assume that if your computer spell-checker doesn't find any errors, the document is error-free. Computers find only words that aren't words; therefore, they miss typos like *form* for *from*.

KEY TWO

Use a thesaurus to find difficult-to-spell words.

If you have no clue as to what letter a word begins with, think of a synonym for it instead. Look up the synonym in the thesaurus. Chances are, the thesaurus will list the word you are looking for and you'll recognize it.

KEY THREE

Write your misspelled words correctly *ten times, saying them aloud as you go.*

You'll not only be using the power of repetition, you'll also benefit from combining sensory input from your eyes (reading), your mouth (speaking), your hand (writing), and your ears (hearing). You'll have a great chance to make a lasting impression on yourself.

 **KEY FOUR**

Isolate your trouble spot in the word and find a gimmick to help you remember.

A great example of this is the word *cemetery*. Or is it *cemetary?* Isolate your trouble spot:

cemet (ae) ry

Here's your gimmick to help you remember:

The word *cemetery* has 3 e's. If you're stuck in a cemetery after midnight, you'd probably be saying "Eee!!"

KEY FIVE

Keep a list of your own troublesome words.

It's much quicker to look up a questionable word on a short list than in a thick dictionary. Just make sure you proofread your list carefully! It's human nature to miss our common misspellings, even when we try hard not to.

54
Syntax

Syntax has to do with sentence *structure*. Are the words of your sentences in the order that will most effectively and clearly communicate your intended message to your listener or reader?

It is vital that you understand one very basic and very important concept of business communication:

The receiver of your message is *busy*.

It is, therefore, your responsibility as the sender to go out of your way to make the intended message clear and easy to grasp.

Awkward sentences, confused sentences, and overly long sentences all contribute to the probability that the receiver will either (1) miss your message or (2) give up before finishing.

The basic English sentence is structured Subject-Verb-Object.

Claudia loves chocolate-covered coffee beans.

      S   V   O

But there are many variations. Again, as long as *clarity* remains your priority, your syntax will more than likely take care of itself.

Pronunciation

Pronouncing words correctly is the burden of the speaker. In fact, correct pronunciation is as important as correct word choice if you want to make a positive professional impact. Mispronounced words are a common image-deflator for many business communicators.

What resources does a speaker have to find out how to pronounce an unfamiliar word? There are many excellent guides to pronunciation—the most obvious is the dictionary. Learn how to read the phonetic alphabet! Accept that dictionaries will occasionally disagree and that depending on the region of the country you reside in, proper pronunciation may differ. If you are speaking to a national audience, the best reference to use is the *NBC Handbook of Pronunciation*. It is the book that broadcasters trust as the "final word" on correct pronunciation.

Here are several commonly mispronounced words. Look them up in the dictionary to find their preferred pronunciations and to familiarize yourself with the phonetic alphabet. Which of the words on the list have more than one acceptable pronunciation?

arctic	heinous
athlete	herb
auxiliary	hibiscus
data	jewelry
debt	lamentable
environment	macro
February	mischievous
government	new
height	nuclear

often	schizophrenia
pianist	species
poinsettia	status
possess	subpoena
prestigious	superfluous
qualm	transient
realtor	twelfth
rhetoric	wash

How to Build the Vocabulary You Need

When you're working to improve your vocabulary, it's important to remember the *purpose* of communication: to clearly and correctly send to a receiver an idea that already exists in *the sender's mind*.

Some people follow the mistaken notion that the more big words they use, the more powerful they are as communicators. But if the purpose of communication is to be *understood* clearly, using a vocabulary full of large, obscure words can have its drawbacks.

Your vocabulary-building goal should be to develop a personal repertoire of words that communicate exact meanings that your receivers will correctly understand.

With this in mind, here are seven keys for developing a truly powerful vocabulary:

1. Establish a personal vocabulary goal.

2. Read with a highlighter.

3. Keep a running list of the words you are learning.

4. Invest the time to learn Latin and Greek root words.

5. Use your developing vocabulary often.

6. Listen closely to others who have a powerful vocabulary.

7. Be yourself.

 **KEY ONE**

Establish a personal vocabulary goal.

Commit to yourself that you are going to learn a certain number of new words each week or month. Then develop a routine for doing it.

Say you decide to learn one new word a day for the next year. Look at your daily schedule. Can you find ten minutes at about the same time every day to devote to the endeavor? Set that time aside and follow through. Within a month, if you are persistent, you will have programmed yourself to easily learn one word each day.

Making a habit of a small but important task is often the best way to ensure you'll stick with it.

 **KEY TWO**

Read with a highlighter.

Do you remember when your teachers told you to read with a dictionary next to you so you could look up the words you didn't understand as you ran across them? Wasn't it difficult to actually *do* that?

Most people find it very impractical to interrupt their reading just to double-check the dictionary for a quick definition. Our brains perceive this as too abrupt an interruption, and maintaining the continuity of what we've read becomes nearly impossible.

If you read with a highlighter in your hand, however, you can highlight a word you're not sure of and *keep reading*. Then, after you've finished the reading, you can review the text and check the meanings of your highlighted words. Or perhaps, once a week you can set aside a few minutes to locate all your highlighted words from the week and look them up then. Of course, an exception to this might be a situation in which not understanding the word would keep you from moving forward. In that case, you would need to look up the word on the spot.

The list you make from these words is an excellent way to get started on a one-word-a-day program.

KEY THREE

Keep a running list of the words you are learning.

Some people like to keep this list in a notebook, with a separate page for each letter of the alphabet. Others keep a small box of index cards, with each word on its own card.

No matter which approach you take, make sure to read through your list quickly at least three times a week. This will help you *remember* the words.

The more often you see these words, the faster you will become comfortable with them and use them. And, of course, the more you use them, the sooner they will become a valuable part of your *natural* vocabulary.

KEY FOUR

Invest the time to learn Latin and Greek root words.

The English language has a colorful past. Its main roots are in Old French and Anglo-Saxon. Actually, though, English contains many, many words not even related to those primary sources.

That's why English is such a difficult language for a nonnative speaker to learn. (Incidentally, it's also what makes spelling such a challenge!)

There are very few shortcuts to learning the English language. But of the few available, here's the one to help you build your usable vocabulary exponentially. Many English words are built around several very popular Latin or Greek roots. Also, many of the prefixes and suffixes we add to words to give them different shades of meaning are rooted in Latin and Greek.

Study the charts included on pages 66 to 69. Notice how easy it becomes to understand some words you aren't familiar with just by dissecting them and deciphering the pieces.

KEY FIVE

Use your developing vocabulary often.

The benefits of using your new words are apparent:

- The more you use them, the more comfortable you'll be with them.

- If you use them incorrectly, you'll probably find out.

- Your communication will become more clear and precise.

Most of us tend to become "addicted" to the words we commonly use and find it hard to think of less used (and probably more specific) substitutes. Think about it. Of the words you understand when reading, how many of them do you find yourself using in conversation?

The words we use to describe with are the ones we most commonly overuse. For example, when someone tells you that "Jack is a *nice* guy," what does that say about Jack? Does it mean Jack is generous, or loyal, or kind, or easy to talk to, or handsome, or funny—or something else? The more vocabulary you use, the more definite and more clear your message will be.

KEY SIX

Listen closely to others who have a powerful vocabulary.

Use your listening time to help you improve your own vocabulary. When you hear someone using a word that you don't often use, and you like the effect it had on you, repeat it to yourself. Repeat the whole sentence—aloud if possible.

This will help you remember that word, and to remember it in context. You'll find yourself using it without even trying to.

KEY SEVEN

Be yourself.

Any communication you send that sounds awkward or unnatural to you will probably also sound that way to your listener. Give yourself time to get comfortable with a new word, but once you've taken that time, if the word doesn't feel right to you, don't feel you must keep using it.

We all have individual personalities—and we *should*. Work hard to make your new vocabulary fit your comfort zone. Use new words over and over. They will work themselves into your natural language—and then you won't even need to think about them.

This is truly the way to clear, precise, and effective communication.

Latin and Greek
Stems, Prefixes, and Suffixes

LATIN STEM	MEANING	EXAMPLE
agr	farm	agriculture
aqua	water	aquatic
cant	sing	cantata
capit	head	capitulate
celer	speed	accelerate
dict	say	dictate
fact	make	factory, perfect
frater	brother	fraternity
greg	group	congregation
jud	right	judge
junct	join	junction
loc	speak	elocution
mand	order	command
mar	sea	maritime
mater	mother	maternity
med	middle	medium
min	lessen	minimum
mort	death	mortal
naut	sailor	nautical
nom	name	nominate
pater	father	paternal
pod	foot	tripod
port	carry	portable
reg	rule	regulation
scrip	write	script
spir	breathe	respiration
tact	touch	tactile
term	end	terminate
vis	see	vision
voc	call	vocation

GREEK STEM	MEANING	EXAMPLE
anthrop	man	morphic
arch	chief, rule	archangel
astron	star	astronomy
auto	self	autobiography
biblio	book	bibliography
bio	life	biochemistry
chrome	color	chromosome
chron	time	chronicle
cosmo	world	cosmos
crat	rule	democratic
dynam	power	dynamo
ge	earth	geological
gen	origin, people	genetics
graph	write	seismograph
gyn	woman	gynecology
homo	same	homonym
hydr	water	hydration
iso	equal	isobar
logy	study of	sociology
macro	large	macroeconomics
meter	measure	barometer
micro	small	microeconomics
mono	one	monogamous
onomy	science	astronomy
onym	name	antonym
pathos	feeling	psychopath
philo	love	philosophy
phobia	fear	agoraphobia
phone	sound	phonics
pseudo	false	pseudonym
psych	mind	psychology
scope	see	periscope
soph	wisdom	sophomore
tele	far off	telephone
theo	god	theosophy
thermo	heat	thermal

Latin and Greek

PREFIXES	MEANING	EXAMPLE
ab, a	away from	abnormal, asexual
ad, ac, at	to	admit, accept, attach
an	without	anorexia
ante	before	antedate
anti	against	antithesis
bene	well	benevolent
bi	two	bicycle
circum	around	circumlocution
com	together	communion
contra	against	contrary
de	from, down	demand
di	apart	divide
ex	out	ex-husband
extra	beyond	extraordinary
in, im, il, ir, un	not	incompetent, imperfect, illegal, irresistible, unlawful
inter	between	interview
intra, intro	within	intramural, introduce
mal	bad	malaise
mis	wrong	mismanaged
non	not	nonsense
ob	against	obsolete
per	through	persist
peri	around	perimeter
poly	many	polymorphic
post	after	posterior
pre	before	prevent
pro	forward	proactive

Latin and Greek (cont.)

PREFIXES	MEANING	EXAMPLE
re	again	reverse
se	apart	sever
semi	half	semiautomatic
sub	under	submarine
super	above	supernatural
sui	self	suicide
trans	across	transport
vice	instead of	viceroy (literally, the vice-king)

Latin and Greek

SUFFIXES	MEANING	EXAMPLE
able, ible	capable of being	portable, crucible
age	state of	baggage
ance	relating to	arrogance
ary	relating to	library
ate	act	obsfucate
ation	action	incubation
cy	quality	lunacy
ence	relating to	irridescence
er, or	one who	writer, actor
ic	pertaining to	heroic
ious	full of	vicious
ize	to make like	prioritize
ment	result	commitment
ty	condition	reality

The Other 93%: Nonverbal Communication

Think about the last time you had an important discussion with someone. Was it when you asked your boss for a raise? Or when you wanted someone close to you to change his or her behavior? Maybe it was when you needed to communicate some less-than-great news to your employees after hearing it from upper management.

Whatever the situation was, think about how you prepared for the talk. Did you spend most of your time planning the words you would use, the tone of voice you would speak in, or the way you would move your body and your face while you were talking?

Most communicators presented with this question laugh. Then they say they thought most about *the words* they would use (of course). But that's why so many times these important communication situations don't turn out the way the thoughtful communicator intended.

Certainly, the *words* are important. They *do* deserve careful consideration. It's just that in any communication exchange in which the parties can both see *and* hear each other, the nonverbal messages that vocal quality and body language send speak much louder than words. The statistic most commonly quoted puts the impact of the *words* at only 7 percent. The *vocal quality* (tone of voice, pace of speech, and so forth) transmits 38 percent of the message. And *body language* (including everything from posture, facial expression, and gestures to the territorial space the listener provides) accounts for a whopping 55 percent of the message the listener receives.

Let's test these numbers.

Imagine that an acquaintance of yours has just entered your office. He stands just inside the door, putting him a good 15 feet away from you. He crosses his arms in front of his chest, slumps his posture a bit, looks at the floor, and sighs deeply. As he speaks, you notice his pitch is about an octave lower than his usual tone and he's speaking very slowly, without inflection.

"I'm delighted about your promotion," he says.

DO YOU REALLY THINK SO??????

The nonverbal messages we send are *essential* to our receivers' understanding of our messages. Unfortunately, for most of us, those nonverbal messages are totally subconscious—they just show up.

In this chapter, we will analyze and discuss the development of conscious, *powerful,* and clear vocal and physical cues that will help you more accurately convey your intended message. Your body language must match your vocal quality, and the two of these together must match the words you speak. This is called *congruency* in communication.

Body Language

There are six keys to body language that you must master if you hope to become a master of communication:

1. Facial expression
2. Posture or stance
3. Gestures and movements
4. Eye contact
5. Territorial space
6. Touch

KEY ONE

Facial expression.

How you hold your face while you are talking *and* listening is incredibly important to the impression both you and your message make on your communication partners.

Try this experiment:

Don't be happy; don't be sad. Just get your totally *neutral* facial expression. Great. Okay, keep it just as it is and find a mirror. Look at yourself and answer the following question:

Do you *really* look neutral *to you?* (It's okay to laugh now.)

Once most people get a chance to *see* their own neutral expressions, they immediately notice that they don't look neutral at all. Many people report that they think their expression actually looks bored. Many others think they look angry. And there are a few who find other words: amused, discontented, tired, or just downright dippy.

The reason our neutral expressions *are* our neutral expressions is that our faces don't have to make any effort to produce them—our facial muscles are slack. They feel great on the inside—we don't even notice them. But our goal is not to communicate with ourselves—it is to communicate with others. It pays to spend some time working with your facial expression.

Play in front of a mirror. Find a facial expression that's not much different from your old neutral one, but friendlier or more open. Practice it. Practice it enough that you can produce it without the mirror, so that you know exactly what it feels like on the inside of your face. (You don't want to have to be checking a mirror in the middle of your next job interview or marriage proposal!)

KEY TWO

Posture or stance.

Have you ever wondered what people thought of you the first time they met you? Do you know that most first impressions are formed within the opening five seconds?

The way you hold your body has an incredibly powerful influence on how other people read you. And the reading they get is usually not even conscious—they couldn't tell you how they came up with it. It's just a "feeling," they'd tell you.

How do you stand? Sit? With one other person? In a small group? In a large group? Do women and men need different stances? Do different messages require different postures?

All these questions need answers—personal answers that work for you.

Find a friend to help you see your posture. Do you remember that game you played when you were a kid, the one where you impersonated everything someone did, as though you were that person's mirror? That's what you're after here.

Ask your friend to stand about six to eight feet away from you and imitate your physical stance and any movements you make. Then try out your normal posture. And experiment with others. See how they look to you. To get an even more accurate reading, start discussing something that bores you to death, and watch what happens to your posture. Then change the subject to something exciting…confidential…funny…and now something that you believe in with all your heart and soul. What kinds of changes did you see in your posture? What did you learn about your effectiveness?

Repeat the same exercise while you are seated, both behind a desk or table and in open space. Find the postures that communicate assertiveness, confidence, and openness—or whatever qualities you would like to project.

KEY THREE

Gestures and movements.

To be an effective communicator, the most important quality you must remember as you make gestures and move is certainly *congruency*. Your gestures and movements need to match the words you say. If they don't, your words don't have a chance. Your listeners will almost always trust what they see before they believe what they *hear*.

Another consideration to keep in mind is the *size* of your gestures. Are they too small or too large for the situation?

Before practicing with your own gestures and movements, spend some time considering what some common gestures mean to you. The following exercise will help you focus your impressions.

EXERCISE 5

The Importance of Gestures and Movements

Listed below are several common gestures and movements people make when they communicate. What do they mean to *you?* Write your first response on the line below each one.

1. You are about to ask your boss for a raise. She crosses her arms in front of her chest and takes a step backward.

   Would you continue with your plan to ask for that raise right now?

   _____

   _____

2. You are seated with a friend, talking about a movie you just saw. Your friend is smiling and leaning toward you, even bouncing a little bit in the chair.

   Does your friend think the movie sounds good?

   _____

   _____

3. You are attending a seminar. As you enter the room, you notice that about half the available seats are still empty. You sit down near another attendee, leaving one chair open between you. The other attendee moves another seat further away.

   _____

   _____

4. Same as #3, except the other attendee moves one seat *closer* to you, not leaving any empty chairs.

_____

_____

5. You tell a co-worker about a problem you are experiencing with a project the two of you share responsibility for. He buries his face in his hands and slowly starts shaking his head from side to side.

   Then you tell your co-worker about the expert consultant the boss gave you authorization to hire to solve the problem. *You* call it—now what does your co-worker do?

_____

_____

As you worked through the exercise, did you notice how easily we tend to interpret body language? The only problem is that sometimes our interpretations are way off base.

Take as an example someone who stands with crossed arms. Perhaps that person isn't closed, or disgusted, or bored. The person may be cold. Or maybe that's just a comfortable stance.

Here's a good rule of thumb for any communicator to follow: When you are the sender, *watch your body language*—take it very seriously. When you are the receiver, notice the body language of the sender, but take it with a grain of salt. Be willing to test it before jumping to conclusions.

Again, using a friend who has agreed to mirror you is the single best way to become aware of what your gestures and movements look like to others. Take the time to practice important communication situations before they really happen. And remember to practice the *nonverbal* aspect too.

KEY FOUR

Eye contact.

Have you ever noticed that when someone speaking to you is making effective eye contact you tend not to question the truth and sincerity of what that person is saying? Have you also noticed how easy it is to get into eye contact trouble?

Surely you've been there. You're in the middle of a conversation, and everything seems to be going well. All of a sudden, the thought crosses your mind that you're not making good eye contact. So you try harder. Oops. Now you're staring. You stop staring. You look to the side. Uh-oh. Now you look bored...what were we talking about?

Here are the four surefire tricks to effective eye contact:

1. *Use the talking head method.* "Talking head" is the term the television industry uses for the video picture of a person from the top of the head to just below the shoulders (just below where the knot of a man's tie would be). It's the way you see newscasters when there's no background video running, just them reading the news.

   If you make general eye contact with the "talking head" area of the person you are speaking with, that person will interpret what you say as sincere and attentive.

2. *In longer exchanges, make very brief pupil-to-pupil eye contact every minute or so.* Very brief means no longer than two seconds.

3. *In much longer exchanges (three minutes and up), glance elsewhere for a brief second every few minutes.* This gives the other person the opportunity to have a moment of privacy.

Have you ever felt like you were caught in a staring contest? Has it ever happened just when you most needed the other person to look away, so you could push a piece of hair out of your eyes or scratch your nose?

Let the other person off the hook occasionally!

4. *Don't let your attention be drawn away by moving hands, environmental distractions, or features not included in the talking head area.* If your communication partner violates this rule, the easiest way to regain that partner's eye contact is to move your hand (or hands) discreetly to the area where your partner's gaze has drifted, then bring your hands back to your face by touching your face or your hair, before returning them to a neutral position. For example, you could swat an imaginary fly away or dust imaginary lint from your clothes.

KEY FIVE

Territorial space.

Have you ever noticed that the distance you define as comfortable is crucial to your ability to participate well in a conversation? Although there are rough guidelines about what is considered to be "safe space" at various levels of relationships, personal taste does account for some variations. Be sensitive to the territorial needs of your communication partners.

As a general rule, people who are intimate (they know most of each other's secrets) tend to be comfortable within three feet of each other for most conversations. Individuals who are friends, but not intimately so, tend to be comfortable anywhere within three to five feet of each other. Acquaintances (social or business) usually prefer a distance of five to eight feet, and people giving presentations generally are at least ten to fifteen feet from the majority of the audience.

Again, these numbers are meant to be used as *general* rules. Certainly when you are traveling outside of the United States and Canada, you'll want to modify these guidelines to accepted practices within your host country. Territorial space needs are extremely dependent upon cultural differences. (It's also interesting to note that natives of crowded cities tend to stand or sit closer to each other than people who live in more open spaces).

In summary, always give your communication partners the space they need to listen and talk with you. You can read their needs by watching their body language (it gets more protective when you get too close) or by noticing whether their conversation becomes more strained or guarded. When your communication partners violate *your* space, consider letting them know—appropriately. (See Chapter 8, "Responsible Assertiveness.")

KEY SIX

Touch.

Should you touch the people you communicate with?

Certainly the answer to that question depends on many factors: the nature of the relationship, the content of the message, and the ability of your communication partner to understand the touch as it was intended are just a few.

In your personal and social relationships, you probably know whether touching is appropriate. In business relationships, use extra caution.

Have you ever known a "hugger"? Perhaps you are one yourself. Hugging is a great idea in many situations, but it needs a vital disclaimer. A person who *does not* want a hug will always be much more offended at getting one than a person who *does* want a hug would be at not getting one. This is especially true in business relationships.

Instead, practice your adeptness at the "One Safe Touch." In business, it is a handshake. A good handshake should be firm, comfortable, dry, and two to three shakes long. Most good business handshakes require only one hand (save two for sympathy) and never cause noticeable movement in the other person's shoulder.

Practice your handshake with everyone you can find who is willing to give you some honest feedback. While you're at it, practice some poor handshakes too. They'll help educate you about your better ones. Incidentally, there are no longer any rules about men/women handshakes. A woman does not need to wait for the man to extend his hand first, and men should shake women's hands in the same way they shake men's hands.

As for other questions of touch in business, use your best judgment, always favoring your most conservative thought. Again, *unwanted touch* will ruin your relationships more quickly than any other nonverbal message.

Vocal Quality—Your Other Nonverbal Consideration

The way your voice sounds as you speak, including its pitch, its volume, and its pace, strongly supports the message you send with your body language. And when you are speaking on the phone, your vocal quality *is* your body language.

What are your vocal habits? Does your pitch go down when you are tired? Does it go up when you get emotional? How about your volume? Do you speak louder when you are excited? Softer when you are bored or fearful? And pace? Do you notice that you speak more quickly under pressure? When you are excited? Nervous?

Discover your vocal habits. The following exercise will help you determine what your voice is presently trained to do—not that you took the time to consciously train it to do these things, of course. But they are your speech *habits*.

Notice that the exercise contains two copies of the worksheet. The first one is for *you* to fill out, the second one is for someone close to you to fill out *about you*. It is often quite helpful to obtain someone else's perspective when dealing with behaviors and vocal cues that you might take for granted.

EXERCISE 6

My Speech Habits

Use this log sheet over the period of a week, making notes on your speech habits as you experience different emotional and physical states. Pay particular attention to your pitch, volume, and pace.

1. When I am TIRED:

Pitch:	High	Normal	Low
Volume:	High	Normal	Low
Pace:	High	Normal	Low

   Other comments: _____

   _____

   _____

   _____

2. When I am ANGRY:

Pitch:	High	Normal	Low
Volume:	High	Normal	Low
Pace:	High	Normal	Low

   Other comments: _____

   _____

   _____

   _____

3. When I am FRUSTRATED:

Pitch: High   Normal   Low

Volume: High   Normal   Low

Pace: High   Normal   Low

Other comments: _____

_____

_____

_____

4. When I am HAPPY:

Pitch: High   Normal   Low

Volume: High   Normal   Low

Pace: High   Normal   Low

Other comments: _____

_____

_____

_____

5. When I am OVERJOYED:

Pitch: High   Normal   Low

Volume: High   Normal   Low

Pace: High   Normal   Low

Other comments: _____

_____

_____

_____

6. When I am feeling POWERFUL:

   Pitch: High   Normal   Low

   Volume: High   Normal   Low

   Pace: High   Normal   Low

   Other comments: _____

   _____

   _____

   _____

7. When I am feeling AFRAID:

   Pitch: High   Normal   Low

   Volume: High   Normal   Low

   Pace: High   Normal   Low

   Other comments: _____

   _____

   _____

   _____

8. When I am feeling SUCCESSFUL:

   Pitch: High   Normal   Low

   Volume: High   Normal   Low

   Pace: High   Normal   Low

   Other comments: _____

   _____

   _____

   _____

9. When I am feeling STRESSED:

Pitch:	High	Normal	Low
Volume:	High	Normal	Low
Pace:	High	Normal	Low

Other comments: _____

_____

_____

_____

10. When I am feeling (ADD YOUR OWN):

Pitch:	High	Normal	Low
Volume:	High	Normal	Low
Pace:	High	Normal	Low

Other comments: _____

_____

_____

_____

_____'s Speech Habits
(fill in name)

Use this log sheet over the period of a week, making notes on your friend's speech habits as he or she experiences different emotional and physical states. In particular, note changes in pitch, volume, and pace.

1. When he/she is TIRED:

   Pitch: High   Normal   Low

   Volume: High   Normal   Low

   Pace: High   Normal   Low

   Other comments: _____

   _____

   _____

   _____

2. When he/she is ANGRY:

   Pitch: High   Normal   Low

   Volume: High   Normal   Low

   Pace: High   Normal   Low

   Other comments: _____

   _____

   _____

   _____

3. When he/she is FRUSTRATED:

Pitch:	High	Normal	Low
Volume:	High	Normal	Low
Pace:	High	Normal	Low

Other comments: _____

_____

_____

_____

4. When he/she is HAPPY:

Pitch:	High	Normal	Low
Volume:	High	Normal	Low
Pace:	High	Normal	Low

Other comments: _____

_____

_____

_____

5. When he/she is OVERJOYED:

Pitch:	High	Normal	Low
Volume:	High	Normal	Low
Pace:	High	Normal	Low

Other comments: _____

_____

_____

_____

6. When he/she is feeling POWERFUL:

Pitch:	High	Normal	Low
Volume:	High	Normal	Low
Pace:	High	Normal	Low

Other comments: _____

_____

_____

_____

7. When he/she is feeling AFRAID:

Pitch:	High	Normal	Low
Volume:	High	Normal	Low
Pace:	High	Normal	Low

Other comments: _____

_____

_____

_____

8. When he/she is feeling SUCCESSFUL:

Pitch:	High	Normal	Low
Volume:	High	Normal	Low
Pace:	High	Normal	Low

Other comments: _____

_____

_____

_____

9. When he/she is feeling STRESSED:

Pitch: High   Normal   Low

Volume: High   Normal   Low

Pace: High   Normal   Low

Other comments: _____

_____

_____

_____

10. When he/she is feeling (ADD YOUR OWN):

Pitch: High   Normal   Low

Volume: High   Normal   Low

Pace: High   Normal   Low

Other comments: _____

_____

_____

_____

Now that you have evaluated where you are in terms of your speech habits, let's take a look at some ways to get where you'd like to be.

Look back over your worksheet. Does your voice tend to change in situations where you wish it wouldn't? Would you like to keep a lower, softer, more moderate vocal quality even when your physical or emotional state is not suggesting it?

Here are some keys:

1. Breathe.

2. Practice your timing.

3. Practice all your important communication exchanges beforehand, when possible.

4. Take a time out if necessary.

5. Note your progress.

KEY ONE

Breathe.

Not only will taking in oxygen help you relax a little bit, it will also automatically give you the breath support you need to speak with more control and to lower your pitch.

... Not to mention the oxygen your brain can use to think clearly, of course.

KEY TWO

Practice your timing.

Start by listening carefully to your favorite comedians. It's their timing that makes them funny, just as your timing contributes most to the impact of your message. When you hear a funny or touching or thought-provoking line, repeat it (under your breath, if necessary) just as the speaker did. By saying it yourself, you will feel the timing that caused you to be moved. And it will be available to you for your own words later.

In general, brief silence before and brief silence after your most important points underlines those points in a very powerful way. (It is *silence* in the middle of speech that gets the listener's attention—not more speaking.)

 **KEY THREE**

Practice all your important communication exchanges beforehand, when possible.

Have a trusted friend serve as your personal vocal coach. Not only will you benefit from that friend's input, but practicing will reinforce in your own mind the way you want to sound.

 **KEY FOUR**

Take a time out if necessary.

If you feel yourself losing control, use an exit line (prewritten for emergencies like this) and give yourself a chance to recover. Your relationships are *too important* to ruin because you didn't have time to think.

Two rules:

1. Once you use an exit line, write a new one to take its place. You need to have a minimum of five escape lines available for your use at all times.

2. Be sure that your exit lines include an appointment to finish the discussion at a definite time (preferably within 24 hours). This will give you the reputation of being a poised *and* responsible communicator.

Example: (Looking at watch) "Wow! Eleven o'clock already? I promised Harry I'd call him at 10:45. He's probably waiting by the phone—I'll be back in 10 minutes and we'll finish this."

KEY FIVE

Note your progress.

Keep the journal recommended in Chapter 1 and remind yourself how well you're doing. Making new habits, especially habits that will take the place of lifelong habits, takes perseverance. Keep on keeping on!

Chapter SEVEN

'Tis Better to Be Heard—Powerful Listening Skills

It's been said that there's a good reason human beings have two ears but only one mouth—that we would all do much better if we'd spend twice as much time listening as we spend talking.

Certainly, being a good listener is a skill all speakers wish upon their listeners. But for people living in a usually busy, sometimes stressful, and always information-packed world, truly great listening skills often come only as an afterthought.

It's time to change that pattern.

Before you read any further, take the Good Listener Quiz in Exercise 7.

Are You a Good Listener?

A. List the last five people you spoke with.

1. _____

2. _____

3. _____

4. _____

5. _____

B. Now, for each person you listed, write down three pieces of information you received and *how* you received it (through words, body language, or vocal quality). Be as specific as possible.

Here's an example:

Person: I spoke with my daughter Eleanor while I was dropping her off at school.

1. She is excited about her violin recital tonight. She said so, she was very animated and talkative, and she was talking very fast about *everything*.

2. She doesn't like her substitute teacher as well as her regular teacher. She *said* she did, but her pitch lowered, her face tilted down and her pace slowed. When I mentioned that her regular teacher would be back the next day, her face came back up, her pitch came back up, and she started talking faster again.

3. She wants to join the Girl Scouts. She pointed out her classmates who were wearing their uniforms today and told me all about what they do in Girl Scouts. Then she asked me how much money it cost to be one. Then she said she thinks she looks really great in green. Then she reminded me how diligent she is with her violin practicing. Then in the sweetest little plaintive voice she could find, she asked if she could join.

Now you try:

Person #1

1. _____

_____

2. _____

_____

3. _____

_____

Person #2

1. _____

_____

2. _____

_____

3. _____

_____

Person #3

1. _____

_____

2. _____

_____

3. _____

_____

Person #4

1. _____

_____

2. _____

_____

3. _____

_____

Person #5

1. _____

_____

2. _____

_____

3. _____

_____

Could you remember three things in each case? Are they the same three things that the people you were writing about would have listed as the three most important things they said to you? Probably not on both counts.

So, why *do* so many people find it difficult to listen well?

Actually, the reasons are quite human—here are the top five:

1. **Distractions.** Both personal and environmental distractions can become a problem for even the most well-meaning communicator. When we have lots on our *own* minds before entering a conversation, it becomes a challenge to listen to the other person with anywhere close to full attention. There's so much noise spinning around in our own heads! Or perhaps the distractions are environmental: loud noises, poor light, uncomfortable chairs, wrong room temperature, and interruptions, to name a few.

2. **Poor speaking skills.** Sometimes the sender makes the listening difficult. Poor speech habits such as mumbling, murmuring, whining, lack of inflection, poor eye contact, poor body language, and use of inappropriate words all interfere powerfully with a listener's ability to accurately decode the message.

3. **Listener's preconceptions.** If the listener enters the conversation with too many preconceptions, it will become impossible for that listener to accurately hear and understand the speaker. This is a result of human psychology—the Theory of Cognitive Dissonance, to be exact. This theory states that once we make up our minds, we become *invested* in our thoughts. We actually subconsciously edit anything we see or hear to prove ourselves right.

4. **Talking is slow.** At least, compared to listening it is! It's *always* easier (and quicker) for listeners to think their way to the speaker's "logical" conclusion than for the speaker to actually think of the words, then form them, and finally, speak them. This leads to lapses in listening. Without careful vigilance, the listener can lose interest during these lapses.

5. **Lack of interest.** In this case, for one reason or another, the listener is just not motivated to pay attention. (This is not always bad.) Perhaps the listener has more important priorities at that moment. If this is the case, the listener should attempt to reschedule the conversation. Or maybe the speaker is speaking to the inappropriate person. If so, the listener should politely redirect the speaker.

We're all busy people—both speakers and listeners. Just remember that a little listening goes a long way in building bridges in relationships. Consider that even if a particular speaker is not discussing something interesting to you today, a small investment of your time can build a lasting rapport that will ease all future contacts with that speaker.

Certainly, becoming a great listener is not a skill that is developed overnight—it takes practice.

Here, then, are the six keys to effective listening:

1. Tune in.

2. Ask for an overview statement.

3. Take notes.

4. Notice the speaker's delivery style, but don't take it too seriously.

5. Repeat the message back to the speaker in your own words.

6. Take a moment to consider—before responding.

KEY ONE

Tune in.

When someone starts talking to you, turn away from as many of the other activities you are engaging in as possible. For example, turn off the television or push the pile of invoices to the side of your desk. Turn your body to face the speaker.

Then give that speaker a positive, open facial expression that encourages him or her to talk.

KEY TWO

Ask for an overview statement.

An overview statement helps both of you—it lets you know what to listen for, and it helps the speaker stay on track. If the speaker hasn't given you an overview statement within the first few minutes, politely interrupt and ask for one. A polite way of handling this might be, "Hey, Jon, I'm glad you stopped in—what points do we need to cover?"

Then, as Jon lists the points, jot them down. This will serve as an outline you can use to keep him on track.

Here are some lines you might use to keep the discussion moving: "Is that everything about the convention? What do we need to discuss about the new office building?"

KEY THREE

Take notes.

Carry a day planner that has note pages in it, and always have note paper available at your desk. When someone starts talking, make a point of recording the most important points. This helps you in three ways:

- It becomes harder for you to be distracted by the delivery style when you are concentrating on the content.

- It slows down your brain, so you don't jump to (dangerous) conclusions.

- It makes the speaker feel good that you care enough to take notes.

KEY FOUR

Notice the speaker's delivery style, but don't take it too seriously.

This goes back to the discussion of nonverbal communication. Certainly, whether the speaker looks you in the eye, whether the speaker's vocal quality is congruent with the message, and how the speaker's body language is looking may hold lots of information for you. Then again, it may not. Maybe this person is just a poor speaker, not insincere. Be sure you don't miss the verbal message—you can evaluate its integrity later, as you weigh the nonverbal cues.

 **KEY FIVE**

Repeat the message back to the speaker in your own words.

Make sure that your understanding of the message matches the speaker's intention. Occasionally, sum up for the speaker what you heard. And, of course, encourage that speaker to clarify the message if you are off-base.

KEY SIX

Take a moment to consider—before responding.

For most of us, this is the toughest guideline of all. It is so easy to use our listening time to plan our own response—but that's not communication. Communication means the transfer of information, not just the speaking of information into a vacuum.

Your listening skills will certainly improve measurably if you practice these six keys, and if you make yourself aware of the five listening trouble spots most people encounter. On the next page, you will find an exercise that will help you through your important listening situations.

Remember, the result of great listening skills is great relationships. The time it takes you to develop this skill is the best investment you can make in your communication style.

EXERCISE 8

Listening to Build Relationships

Use this checklist before, during, and after your important listening situations. It will help you to focus on the skills you'll need to master in order to become a more effective listener.

Before the event

1. What are my feelings about the speaker?

2. What are my thoughts, assumptions, and feelings about the topic?

3. What do I expect from this event?

4. What's going on in my life and in my head that could get in the way of good listening skills in this situation?

During the event

1. Acknowledge my preconceptions and mental busy-ness (see #4 above), but put them behind me.

2. Tune in: Pay special attention to eye contact and body language.

3. What is the speaker's overview statement? Make sure the speaker states it. If not, remember to ask.

4. Take notes!

5. Be aware of the speaker's changing nonverbal messages— but keep taking notes.

6. Summarize for the speaker what I heard him or her say.

7. Allow the speaker to correct and clarify.
8. Breathe.
9. Then respond.
10. End the encounter on a positive or light note, if possible.

After the event

1. How did it go?
2. What did I do well?
3. Where could I improve?
4. Is there any action I need to take?
5. When will I follow up with this speaker to continue to build a positive relationship?

Chapter
EIGHT

Responsible Assertiveness

Assertiveness is standing up for your personal rights and acting in ways that express your thoughts, feelings, and beliefs directly, honestly, and appropriately without violating another person's rights.

That's quite a definition to take in, isn't it?

Actually, there's one word in that definition that's much more important than the others. Get a red pen right now and circle the word *appropriately*.

Appropriate assertiveness is what makes the difference between assertiveness that works and assertiveness that can get you in trouble. Certainly, honesty is always the best policy—when it works. Sometimes, however, it benefits us (and the future of our relationships) to consider the receiver's needs, feelings, and likely reactions.

For example, have you ever received some kind of assertiveness training? If so, while you were in that classroom, didn't it sound like a *great* idea? So you took it home and to work. Maybe you tried it out on a spouse or a boss. Did it go as well as you had been promised?

All too often, it doesn't. The spouse's feelings get hurt. Or the boss goes into a rage.

What happened? More than likely, the crucial issue of appropriateness was lacking.

Responsible assertiveness takes into consideration the receiver's feelings and needs. It's *always* better to maintain as positive a relationship as possible with all the people we associate with—to do otherwise would be to burn bridges.

Here, then, are the eight keys to responsible assertiveness:

1. Do your homework.

2. Start with the evidence procedure.

3. Use the word *think* instead of *feel*.

4. Mention feelings, if it's appropriate.

5. Describe, in objective ways, what you want.

6. Ask for the receiver's feedback.

7. Negotiate, if necessary.

8. Maintain goodwill with the other person, apart from your current exchange.

KEY ONE

Do your homework.

Never try to be properly assertive on the spur of the moment. You're destined to fail. Most of us do not actually mention a disturbing behavior or action to the "perpetrator" until we are slightly *more* than annoyed by it. By that time, the behavior is carrying an emotional charge for us. It is difficult to remain neutral (i.e., not aggressive) when we are emotionally charged. Instead, we have a tendency to get carried away and to say things that we later wish we hadn't.

When you feel the need to be assertive with someone, always spend at least twenty minutes going over your words and actions beforehand. If possible, try your plan out on someone else first, so that any aggressive body language or vocal quality will get picked up by that person—and not by your genuine receiver. Exercise 9 on page 127 will help you.

KEY TWO

Start with the evidence procedure.

Has anyone ever approached you and said something that started like this: "Obviously, you…"

Perhaps it was, "Obviously, you don't care about me anymore." Or maybe, "Obviously, you don't care about finishing the filing I gave you to do." Have you ever heard that?

What is your first response when someone starts with a *judgment* of you? Is it agreeable? Probably not. Isn't it more like, "Right on, Sherlock—I don't!"

Most people respond to an attack *defensively*—and for many that means *aggressively*. Obviously, this is not the best way to maintain a relationship.

Instead, start with the evidence procedure. When you decide it's time to get assertive, you must become like a good attorney building a case. What are the objective criteria, the evidence that anyone could see, that will prove your point. State those items first. But do it in a neutral way, like this:

"I notice there is a stack of filing on your desk that appears to be close to two inches high. As a matter of fact, it bears a remarkable resemblance to the stack of filing I gave you three weeks ago. I see that it is 11:00 a.m. And I see you are reading *Cosmopolitan* at your desk."

From here, notice that a logical jump will be to say: "This all makes me think that my filing isn't a high priority for you today."

But because you started with the evidence, maybe the situation will straighten itself out. Maybe your secretary will say: "You're right—this stack *does* bear a remarkable resemblance to that stack you gave me three weeks ago. But actually, I filed your stack *then*. This is a stack I just got from my *other* boss, and as if that isn't bad enough, she also has me reading these stupid magazines trying to find every reference I can to dental hygiene!"

KEY THREE

Use the word think *instead of the word* feel.

Have you ever been emotionally blackmailed? The most common technique experienced blackmailers use is to say the words "I feel..." as often as possible.

"I feel you just don't care about us..."

"I feel you don't care about my filing."

"I feel the world is an unkind place."

"I feel you should know better."

Yet there is no emotion on earth called "you just don't care about us," or "the world is an unkind place," or even "you should know better." All of those statements are *thoughts,* not *feelings.* They should be labeled correctly:

"I think you just don't care..."

"I think the world is an unkind place."

"I think you should know better."

When you use honest language, your receiver can sense that, even if he or she disagrees with your message. There is more respect, both ways.

KEY FOUR

Mention feelings, if it's appropriate.

In some of your relationships, you will want to acknowledge your emotions. But be assertive; take ownership. It's just not assertive to say, "You make me so mad." In fact, always word your emotional statements from the "I" perspective. "I'm feeling angry" is much better than "I'm angry." Do you see the difference?

You may be tall, or you may be a redhead, but you are *not* angry. Personifying emotions is dangerous. Would you really want to be the embodiment of anger? Or of any other emotion? "I *feel* angry" allows you to stop feeling that way at some point and to feel something more productive.

There is an interesting point about freedom here, too. When you believe that someone else has had the power to make you angry, then you've made that person your jailer. When you believe that you own your emotions and that you are responsible for them, then you have the key to your cell.

KEY FIVE

Describe, in objective ways, what you want.

Most assertiveness is an attempt to change the receiver's thoughts, actions, attitudes, or feelings. Once you have explained the evidence (Key #2), expressed your thoughts, and if appropriate, your feelings about that evidence (Keys #3 and #4), you generally want to encourage a change. "I'd like you to complete this filing." Or "I'd like you to act more like you care about me."

When making these statements, you must remain vigilant. You must have an evidence procedure here too.

- "I'd like the filing to be completed by 2:00 tomorrow afternoon." But make sure you share a meaning for "completed" with the receiver before you walk away.

- Or "I'd like you to call me from work a few times a week. And I'd like you to bring me presents when you go out of town. And I'd like you to give me a back rub when I get home from work."

In both of these examples, at least the receiver knows clearly what you define as "filing efficiency" or "caring more about me."

KEY SIX

Ask for the receiver's feedback.

Wouldn't life be simple if you could dictate to other people exactly what you wanted at all times and they would provide it—with a smile?

Of course, such is not the case. When communicating responsibly, you may need to negotiate—and the first step to successful negotiation is to *listen*. When you are listening to the feedback you get, make sure the receiver stays objective too. If the receiver lists some of his or her wishes, make sure there is a clear evidence procedure so that there won't be a broken agreement later on.

KEY SEVEN

Negotiate, if necessary.

Brainstorm a list of all possible ways you could settle a disagreement or a conflict with another person. If necessary, agree to try some of these alternatives on a trial-and-error basis before choosing a final answer.

When both parties are committed to a single solution from the beginning, it puts too much pressure on them and discourages them from giving in here and there. Take the pressure off. Start with more than one solution.

Also, avoid "positional" negotiation. This is a communication technique that pits people against each other: "I'm on the left, you're on the right" or "I'm the parent, you're the child." As you've probably guessed, the Theory of Cognitive Dissonance takes over and total communication becomes impossible. Make it easy for other people to think or feel the way they do: "Gee, I can see how you could think that. But I disagree."

 **KEY EIGHT**

Maintain goodwill with the other person, apart from your current exchange.

Even if your current communication exchange doesn't work out perfectly, be willing to forgive and forget. Keep your mind open to the other valuable qualities of your communication partner, and work to maintain a warm relationship.

This doesn't mean you need to trust someone who has violated your confidence, or to share sensitive information with someone who gossips. But you *do* need to treat all people with respect and courtesy. This is the only way to establish and keep the reputation you want: one of a fair, trustworthy, and respectful communicator.

EXERCISE 9

Responsible Assertiveness Worksheet

Use this worksheet to plan what you want to communicate to the receiver of your assertiveness. Remember to allow at least 20 minutes for this activity *before* you have your conversation.

1. When _____(fill in name)_____ does _____
   (fill in the behavior or thing that is annoying you)

   _____

2. Express how you feel. This will clear your emotional air— let all your emotions out *here*—not on your receiver. I feel

   _____

   _____

   _____

3. What is the evidence procedure you will use? Remember, you are an attorney assembling a hard case.

   _____

   _____

   _____

   _____

   _____

4. What is going on for the receiver in this situation?

   _____

   _____

   _____

5. What really bothers me most about this situation?

_____

_____

_____

6. What do I want to be different about this situation?

_____

_____

Okay, but being reasonable, what do I want to be different?

_____

_____

_____

7. What am I willing to compromise, or to offer in return?

_____

_____

_____

8. What do I like about the receiver? List at least three things.

_____

_____

_____

_____

Responsible Assertiveness Worksheet

Example

Use this worksheet when you are planning what you want to communicate to the receiver of your assertiveness. Remember to allow at least 20 minutes for this activity before you have your conversation.

1. When _____*My office partner*_____ does _____
   (fill in name)

   (fill in the behavior or thing that is annoying you)

   All that loud, disgusting gum-chomping

2. Express how you feel. This will clear your emotional air—
   let all your emotions out here—not on your receiver. I feel

   Furious, disgusted, sick

3. What is the evidence procedure you will use? Remember,
   you are an attorney assembling a hard case.

   She arrives in the morning with fifteen packs of gum.
   By noon, our wastebasket is half full of the wrappers.
   Her mouth moves up and down (and stays open) much of
   the day. A loud slurping noise comes from her side of
   the office most of the day.

4. What is going on for the receiver in this situation?

   She likes gum? She's nervous? She's quit smoking?

5. What really bothers me most about this situation?

My privacy is totally violated, and the noise really disgusts me.

6. What do I want to be different about this situation?

I want my own office! I want her to be fired!

Okay, but being reasonable, what do I want to be different?

I want to not hear that gum slurping most of the day.

7. What am I willing to compromise, or to offer in return?

A few gum-chewing breaks for her throughout the day

8. What do I like about the receiver? List at least three things.

Sense of humor

Has quit smoking

Helps me when I'm overloaded

RESPONSIBLE ASSERTIVENESS CHECKLIST

STEP 1: Do your homework.

- Complete Exercise 9.
- Practice with a friend.
- Pay special attention to nonverbal communication:
    - Body language
    - Vocal quality
- Make adjustments using your friend's feedback.

STEP 2: Start with the evidence procedure.

- Gather the evidence that supports your beliefs in this situation.
    - What do I see?
    - What have I heard? Remember to document!
    - What other *verifiable* sensory data is there?

STEP 3: Use the word "think."

- What judgments have I made because of the data in Step 2?
- Write those judgments down as "I think" statements.

STEP 4: Mention feelings, if appropriate.

- Is expressing my feelings appropriate in this situation?
- What are my feelings?

STEP 5: Describe in objective ways what I want.

- What do I want?
- How can I measure it?
- By when?
- By whom?
- Where?
- How?
- Why?

STEP 6: Ask for the receiver's feedback.

- Listen with an open posture.
- Maintain an open facial expression.
- Read back the other person's comments.

STEP 7: Negotiate, if necessary.

- What's in it for the receiver?
- How many different settlements are possible?
- Which one should we try first?

STEP 8: Maintain goodwill.

- Dump your negative feelings (somewhere else!).
- Make a friendly call to the other person.

Practical Application: Dealing With Difficult Behavior

Plenty of resources are available for dealing with difficult behavior, and certainly this chapter does not intend to take the place of them. Its intent is simply to add the perspective of the thoughtful communicator.

Notice the title of this chapter, in particular the use of the word "behavior" instead of the word "people." Indeed, many books, tapes, and training programs refer to difficult *people,* even going so far as to outline and label all the different types of these people.

Yet a communicator hoping to maintain a positive rapport, which is often crucial to the success of the communication, should consider using a different approach. When we label a person as "difficult," our psychology usually takes over. Remember the Theory of Cognitive Dissonance? It also has applications when it comes to labeling.

Cognitive dissonance theory holds that once the human brain thinks something is true, it works hard to help the brain maintain its belief no matter *what* evidence may show up to the contrary. In other words, once you apply a label, your brain will help you maintain that label with selective listening, selective sight, and selective thought. Only when the evidence contrary to your belief is *overwhelming* will your brain notice that you need to change your mind.

Hmmmmm.

Let's say your mother-in-law calls. She's telling you about her trip to Palm Springs. You mentally apply the label "complainer." The next time she calls, notice whether you have a tendency to *expect* a complaint soon into the conversation.

Maybe your mother-in-law does complain occasionally. Is it doing you any good to label her in advance? Would it be better to simply refer to her as "my mother-in-law who occasionally complains about things." Psychologically, this simple change lets her off of your mental hook and allows you to find other things about her that are perhaps more positive.

Here then is the thoughtful communicator's philosophy about difficult behavior. Use it as your key to dealing effectively with difficult behavior.

1. People experience bouts of difficult behavior. Behavior doesn't make people difficult.

2. A person exhibiting difficult behavior hasn't decided to be difficult—simply to survive or cope.

3. If you allow yourself to react automatically to difficult behavior, you also will be exhibiting difficult behavior.

4. All difficult behavior is rooted in fear.

5. Well-considered communication is the only effective way to dealing with fear.

KEY ONE

People experience bouts of difficult behavior. Behavior doesn't make people difficult.

Notice that this point involves a change of attitude, not a change of reality. In order to put it into action, all you must do is *decide* to.

People are tall or red-headed, but *not* difficult. Remember?

KEY TWO

A person exhibiting difficult behavior hasn't decided to be difficult—simply to survive or cope.

This contains a complex, yet simple truth. No one gets up in the morning, looks in the mirror and says, "What can I do today to be really *difficult?!?!*" (Okay, okay, *almost* no one.)

People have learned their difficult behavior, very much like Pavlov's dogs learned to salivate at the sound of a bell. Over a period of time, the behavior you may now deem difficult has effectively helped the other person feel in control, or safe, or courageous, or whatever it is that person wanted to feel. Also, it worked to get that person what was wanted often enough that it became *conditioned*.

Little children who whine and get what they want learn how to be adults who whine to get what they want. Little children whose temper tantrums get them the attention they want grow up and yell at other people to get attention. Do you see how this works?

 **KEY THREE**

If you allow yourself to react automatically to difficult behavior, you also will be exhibiting difficult behavior.

This is probably apparent to you. Have you ever been approached by a person who was yelling, so you yelled back? Did it turn into a yelling match? Did either one of you suddenly feel overwhelmed by understanding and love in the middle of the yelling? It's doubtful.

When you react without thinking, you are also exhibiting a conditioned (programmed) response. Is this real communication? Of course not.

 **KEY FOUR**

All difficult behavior is rooted in fear.

This statement can change it all for each of us. The next time someone's difficult behavior is causing you considerable discomfort, interrupt your own programming. Ask yourself: What is this person afraid of right now? If you give yourself the time and the space to be objective, you *will* find an answer. And once you find the fear, you will find it nearly impossible to fall into *your* old pattern of reaction.

If all else fails, visualize yourself writing (with a red felt tip pen) the words "I'm afraid" on the other person's forehead in the middle of *that person's* display of difficult behavior. (Please remember: This is a visualization only.)

KEY FIVE

Well-considered communication is the only way to deal with fear.

This is ultimately what all those other resources provide you with: tips for communicating effectively, for dealing with and coping with other people who are exhibiting difficult behavior. There are different strategies for different behaviors, but they are all based on thoughtful and preconsidered responses.

Here's another key to remember for any communication situation that has become difficult or impossible: Can you take a time out? Simply acknowledging that things have gotten very heated and that maybe you'd both do better after a break can work wonders. Or maybe you need to resort to using an exit line: "Wow! I didn't realize it's so late. Give me five minutes. I've got to call Jane and tell her where I am!"

When you feel one of your buttons being pushed, it's much better for the long-term health of your relationships if you *take the time out*. As human beings, we aren't always going to be rational—especially when our emotions are running the show.

Do yourself a favor. Think of a few of the people with whom you tend to experience some difficulty. Then think of at least three ways to interrupt the difficult moment. It might be the best planning you ever do to preserve your relationships. Use the exercise on the next page to record your ideas.

EXERCISE 10

My Time-Out Strategies

List a few of the people with whom you experience difficult moments. Then, under each name, list at least three (five would be great) ways to interrupt the difficult moment, to buy yourself a moment to think rationally and to determine your course of action.

EXAMPLE:

PERSON: The boss

INTERRUPTIONS:

1. Spill my coffee on the floor

2. Have a coughing attack

3. Hear a ringing phone and say, "Oh, it's (whatever time)—Robin said he'd call back then. I'll be right back!"

4. "Wow, it's (time) already! I promised Jack I'd call 15 minutes ago. Can we finish this in ten minutes? Jack's an important client—I'm uncomfortable keeping him waiting!"

5. Have Mike interrupt us after 5 minutes

PERSON #1: _____

INTERRUPTIONS:

1. _____

2. _____

3. _____

4. _____

5. _____

PERSON #2: _____

INTERRUPTIONS:

1. _____

2. _____

3. _____

4. _____

5. _____

PERSON #3: _____

INTERRUPTIONS:

1. _____

2. _____

3. _____

4. _____

5. _____

And Finally...

What does it take to be a great communicator?

Has the answer to that question become more clear to you as you've worked through this book?

Ultimately, your answer will be personal—tailored for your own needs. But it also pays to consider just what this whole process of communication—the transfer of meaning from one person to another—means to us as a society.

It is our ability to communicate and our willingness to continue refining our skills of communication that have led to every step forward we have taken on this planet.

All progress begins with the sharing of information. And most progress begins humbly—with one person communicating with another.

We no longer live in caves because one person shared information with one other person—who then shared information with another person—and so on and on and on.

Practice the skills you've learned in this book. Work through the exercises. Be willing to have learning experiences and to make mistakes. Be willing to grow!

Your communication skills are the single strongest tool you have available for changing the world—on both a personal level and a global one.

All the best to you as you master them!

Communication Effectiveness Journal

Sample

Who? _____

_____

_____

Goal of Communication: _____

_____

_____

Expected Outcome:_____

_____

_____

Actual Outcome: _____

_____

_____

If I Could Do It All Over, I'd... _____

_____

_____

Notes: _____

_____

_____

_____

_____

_____

_____

Communication Effectiveness Journal

Sample

Who? _co-worker_

Goal of Communication: _____
Get her to stop interrupting me while I'm busy

Expected Outcome: _____
She'll see it my way

Actual Outcome: _____
She got hurt—now she isn't speaking to me

If I Could Do It All Over, I'd... _____
_Think of some benefits for her to do it my
way before I approached her._

Notes: _____
_I like Sally so much...maybe if I communicated that
first, then explained to her how it'd be good for her,
then suggested we have lunch together soon, this
could work out better._

Bibliography and Suggested Resources

BOOKS

Alberti, Robert E., and Michael L. Emmons. *Your Perfect Right: A Guide to Assertive Living,* 6th ed. San Luis Obispo, CA: Impact Publishers, 1990.

Andersen, Richard. *Write It Right!* Mission, KS: SkillPath Publications, 1993.

Andersen, Richard. *Writing That Works: A Practical Guide for Business and Creative People.* New York: McGraw-Hill, 1989.

Bandler, Richard, and John Grinder. *Frogs Into Princes: Neuro Linguistic Programming.* Moab, UT: Real People Press, 1979.

Beckoff, Samuel. *Good English With Ease: A Modern Method for Correcting Your Errors.* New York: Arco Publishing, 1977.

Bone, Diane. *The Business of Listening: A Practical Guide to Effective Listening.* Los Altos, CA: Crisp Publications, 1988.

Brock, Susan L. *Better Business Writing.* Los Altos, CA: Crisp Publications, 1987.

Brown, Rita Mae. *Starting From Scratch: A Different Kind of Writer's Manual.* New York: Bantam Books, 1988.

Caroselli, Marlene. *The Language of Leadership.* Amherst, MA: Human Resource Development Press, 1990.

Caroselli, Marlene. *Meetings That Work.* Mission, KS: SkillPath Publications, 1994.

Clarke, Colleen. *Networking: How to Creatively Tap Your People Resources.* Mission, KS: SkillPath Publications, 1993.

Dudley, Denise M. *Every Woman's Guide to Career Success.* Mission, KS: SkillPath Publications, 1991.

Ehrlich, Eugene, and Raymond Hand. *NBC Handbook of Pronunciation,* 4th ed. rev. New York: Harper & Row, 1991.

Eisenson, Jon. *Voice and Diction: A Program for Improvement,* 3rd ed. New York: Macmillan, 1974.

Elster, Charles Harrington. *There Is No Zoo in Zoology: And Other Beastly Mispronunciations.* London: Collier Macmillan, 1988.

Frank, Milo O. *How to Get Your Point Across in 30 Seconds—or Less.* New York: Simon and Schuster, 1986.

Freeman, Lawrence A., and Terry R. Bacon. *Shipley Associates Style Guide: Writing in the World of Work, rev. ed.* Bountiful, UT: Shipley Associates, 1990.

Friedman, Paul. *How to Deal With Difficult People.* Mission, KS: SkillPath Publications, 1989.

Funk, Peter. *It Pays to Increase Your Word Power*. New York: Bantam Books, 1990.

Henson, Carol, and Thomas L. Means. *Fundamentals of Business Communication*. Cincinnati: South-Western Publishing, 1990.

Laborde, Genie Z. *Fine Tune Your Brain: When Everything's Going Right and What to Do When It Isn't*. Palo Alto, CA: Syntony Publishing, 1988.

Laborde, Genie Z. *Influencing With Integrity: Management Skills for Communication and Negotiation*. Palo Alto, CA: Syntony Publishing, 1983.

Robbins, Anthony. *Unlimited Power*. New York: Fawcett Columbine, 1986.

Shouse, Deborah. *Breaking the Ice: How to Improve Your On-the-Spot Communication Skills*. Mission, KS: SkillPath Publications, 1994.

Walton, Donald W. *Are You Communicating? You Can't Manage Without It*. New York: McGraw-Hill, 1989.

Wells, Gordon. *How to Communicate*. 2nd Edition. New York: McGraw-Hill, 1986.

Zinsser, William K. *On Writing Well: An Informal Guide to Writing Nonfiction*. New York: Perennial Library, 1990.

Audiocassettes

Fremerman, Marvin. *The Dynamics of High Self-Esteem: A Guide for Personal and Professional Growth*. Mission, KS: SkillPath Publications, 1991.

Koehnline, William A. *Winning With Words: Seven Vocabularies for Success*. New York: Nightingale-Conant, 1985.

Nightingale-Conant Corp. *NPL: The New Technology of Achievement*. New York: Nightingale-Conant, 1991.

Poley, Michelle. *Powerful Proofreading and Editing Skills*. Mission, KS: SkillPath Publications, 1990.

Reynolds, Carol. *Managing Your Self-Esteem & Inner Power: An Assertiveness Guide for Women*. Mission, KS: SkillPath Publications, 1990.

Videocassettes

Poley, Michelle. *Eight Steps to Better Business Writing*. Mission, KS: SkillPath Publications, 1994.

Available from SkillPath Publications

Other Resources by Michelle Fairfield Poley

A Winning Attitude: How to Develop Your Most Important Asset! *(Spiral Handbook)*

Eight Steps to Better Business Writing *(Quick-Study Video)*

Powerful Proofreading and Editing Skills *(Set of six audiocassettes)*

Self-Study Sourcebooks

Climbing the Corporate Ladder: What You Need to Know and Do to Be a Promotable Person *by Barbara Pachter and Marjorie Brody*

Mastering the Art of Communication: Your Keys to Developing a More Effective Personal Style *by Michelle Fairfield Poley*

Organized for Success: 95 Tips for Taking Control of Your Time, Your Space, and Your Life *by Nanci McGraw*

Productivity Power: 250 Great Ideas for Being More Productive *by Jim Temme*

Promoting Yourself: 50 Ways to Increase Your Prestige, Power, and Paycheck *by Marlene Caroselli, Ed.D.*

Risk-Taking: 50 Ways to Turn Risks Into Rewards *by Marlene Caroselli, Ed.D. and David Harris*

Total Quality Customer Service: How to Make It Your Way ᴏ. Life *by Jim Temme*

Write It Right! A Guide for Clear and Correct Writing *by Richard Andersen and Helene Hinis*

Spiral Handbooks

The ABC's of Empowered Teams: Building Blocks for Success *by Mark Towers*

Breaking the Ice: How to Improve Your On-the-Spot Communication Skills *by Deborah Shouse*

The Care and Keeping of Customers: A Treasury of Facts, Tips, and Proven Techniques for Keeping Your Customers Coming BACK! *by Roy Lantz*

Dynamic Delegation! A Manager's Guide for Active Empowerment *by Mark Towers*

Every Woman's Guide to Career Success *by Denise M. Dudley*

Hiring and Firing: What Every Manager Needs to Know *by Marlene Caroselli, Ed.D. with Laura Wyeth, Ms.Ed.*

How to Deal With Difficult People *by Paul Friedman*

Learning to Laugh at Work: The Power of Humor in the Workplace *by Robert McGraw*

Making Your Mark: How to Develop a Personal Marketing Plan for Becoming More Visible and More Appreciated at Work *by Deborah Shouse*

Meetings That Work *by Marlene Caroselli, Ed.D.*

The Mentoring Advantage: How to Help Your Career Soar to New Heights *by Pam Grout*

NameTags Plus: Games You Can Play When People Don't Know What to Say *by Deborah Shouse*

Networking: How to Creatively Tap Your People Resources *by Colleen Clarke*

New & Improved! 25 Ways to Be More Creative and More Effective *by Pam Grout*

Power Write! A Practical Guide to Words That Work *by Helene Hinis*

Putting Anger to Work For You! *by Ruth and Joel Schroeder*

Reinventing Your Self: 28 Strategies for Coping With Change *by Mark Towers*

The Supervisor's Guide: The Everyday Guide to Coordinating People and Tasks *by Jerry Brown and Denise Dudley, Ph.D.*

Taking Charge: A Personal Guide to Managing Projects and Priorities *by Michal E. Feder*

Treasure Hunt: 10 Stepping Stones to a New and More Confident You! *by Pam Grout*

A Winning Attitude: How to Develop Your Most Important Asset! *by Michelle Fairfield Poley*

For more information, call 1-800-873-7545.